WRITING AND STAGING

Myths and Legends

Charlotte Guillain

capstone

To contact Capstone Global Library please call 800-747-4992, or visit our web site
www.capstonepub.com

Edited by James Benefield
Designed by Philippa Jenkins
Original illustrations © Capstone Global Library Limited 2016
Picture research by Kelly Garvin
Production by Victoria Fitzgerald
Originated by Capstone Global Library Ltd
Printed and bound in China

19 18 17 16 15
10 9 8 7 6 5 4 3 2 1

Library of Congress Cataloging-in-Publication Data
Cataloging-in-publication data is available at the Library of Congress.
ISBN 978 1 4846 2772 3 (hardback)
ISBN 978 1 4846 2776 1 (paperback)
ISBN 978 1 4846 2780 8 (ebook PDF)

Acknowledgments
Alamy: Hill Street Studios/Blend Images, 27, Luc Novovitch, 7, Mary Evans Picture Library, 11; Capstone Press/ Karon Dubke, cover, 24, 25, 32, 33, 39; Corbis: H. Lorren Au Jr/ZUMA Press, 35, Hulton-Deutsch Collection, 5, Robbie Jack, 38, Robert Wallace, 22, Tomas Rodriguez, 42; Getty Images: Dave M/ Benett, 36, Encyclopedia Britannica/UIG, 4, Peter Cade, 6; Granger, NYC, 10; iStockphoto: 36clicks, 28; Newscom: Kristin Callahan/Ace Pictures, 14, Warner Bros. Pictures, 18; Shutterstock: ID1974, 16, Anton_Ivanov, 26, Igor Bulgarin, 31, James L/ Davidson, 37, Jef Thompson, 12, Pavel L Photos and Video, 20, Stocksnapper, 9; Superstock: Cusp, 34, Hill Street Studios/Blend Images, 43, Ivan Vdovin/age footstock, 23, Steve Vidler, 30; The Image Works: Bob Daemmrich, 19, 40, Nobby Clark/ArenaPal, 29.

Artistic Elements: Shutterstock/3DDock.

We would to thank Mike Gould for his invaluable help with this book.

CONTENTS

What Is a Myth or Legend?...............4

What Is a Play? 6

Plays Based on Myths
    and Legends....................10

A Beginning, Middle, and End..........16

Who's in Charge? 20

Acting in a Play Based on a
    Myth or Legend 24

Behind the Scenes 28

Portraying the Minotaur.................32

The Final Stages 38

Showtime!....................................... 42

Glossary 44

Find Out More................................... 46

Index.. 48

Some words are shown in bold,
like this. You can find out what they
mean by looking in the glossary.

WHAT IS A MYTH OR LEGEND?

For thousands of years, humans have shared stories with one another. To begin with, stories were told by **oral** storytellers and were passed down through the generations before they were written down. Some of the oldest stories we know are **myths** and **legends**.

A myth is an old, traditional story that is not based on real events. Many myths started in ancient civilizations such as in Greece, China, or Egypt. They are often about gods and goddesses or brave human heroes with special powers. Myths from different cultures often explain how people believe the world began and how it works. A famous Greek myth is the story of King Midas, who wished that everything he touched would turn to gold.

Like myths, many legends are set hundreds or thousands of years ago and have been passed on by storytellers over the years. Unlike myths, legends are originally based on people or events that really existed or took place. The story may have been changed over time to teach people something, make them obey their rulers, or give a special message.

King Midas also turned people into gold.

4

Some people believe that the legend of King Arthur was based on a real person.

While a legend may include real facts from human history, it can also involve mythical creatures such as dragons and giants. The legend of King Arthur is a famous example.

These wonderful stories have been told in many different ways over the centuries. One good way to share myths and legends is to perform them in a play.

The Vikings had their own myths involving gods and monsters, known as Norse mythology. Many days of the week in English-speaking countries are named after Norse gods and goddesses. For example:

Tuesday: Named after Tyr, god of war and glory
Wednesday: Named after Woden (also known as Odin), chief of the gods
Thursday: Named after Thor, god of thunder
Friday: Named after Freya, goddess of love and war

WHAT IS A PLAY?

A play is a story that is acted out on a stage in front of an audience. There are many people involved in creating and staging a play. The actors who perform onstage are the most visible members of the team, but every play starts with a **script**, written by a **playwright**. A **director** is then needed to organize everyone involved, including all the people who work behind the scenes. Staging a play can take weeks or months of preparation, but it is worth all the hard work!

Where are plays performed?

Plays can be performed in all sorts of places, from famous theaters to community centers or school auditoriums. Some plays are performed outdoors, in open-air theaters or **amphitheaters**, or even in someone's backyard! Plays can have long and complicated stories, or they can be about a short and simple event.

You could rehearse your play in a classroom at school.

American Indians sometimes share their own legends through performance. You can perform these, too.

People put on plays in professional theaters, where famous actors perform and the audience can pay a lot of money for tickets. However, many plays are also performed by **amateur** theater groups as a hobby.

Many schools put on plays, with students taking part in onstage and backstage activities. It can be an amazing shared experience for everyone involved.

Many movies are based on myths or legends. For example, the *Percy Jackson* books and movies involve characters based on gods and heroes from Greek mythology, the animated movie *Mulan* is based on an ancient Chinese legend, and Norse gods and monsters are mentioned in the *How to Train Your Dragon* books and movies.

The script of a play

The words, or **lines,** that actors speak in a play form the **dialogue** in a script, created by the playwright. A play script is different than a movie or television script since it is written for a live performance on a stage.

It is the actors' job to tell the story by acting out the dialogue in a script. By looking for their characters' names—which appear down the left-hand side of the page in the script—the actors will know when it is their turn to speak. Each character's lines appear after his or her name, like this:

Drama was very popular in ancient Greece. Some famous ancient Greek playwrights include Sophocles, Aristophanes, and Euripides. Their plays were usually about heroes and gods. There were **tragedies** where the characters suffer terrible events, and **comedies,** which are funny plays written to make people laugh.

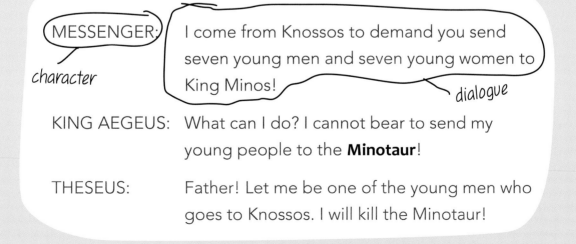

MESSENGER: I come from Knossos to demand you send seven young men and seven young women to King Minos!

character

dialogue

KING AEGEUS: What can I do? I cannot bear to send my young people to the **Minotaur**!

THESEUS: Father! Let me be one of the young men who goes to Knossos. I will kill the Minotaur!

The actors' lines and characters' names are not the only words on the pages of a play script. There are also **stage directions**. These are instructions telling the actors how to speak or move at different moments in the play. They are usually in italics and parentheses (*like this*), to stand out from the characters' lines. For example:

KING AEGEUS: (*horrified*) I cannot let you go, Theseus!

stage direction

THESEUS: (*kneeling before Aegeus*) You must. Only I, the king's son, can destroy this monster and save the sons and daughters of Athens.

KING AEGEUS: (*weeping*) I pray to the gods that you will return safely.

Sophocles, pictured here, wrote famous tragedies, such as *Antigone* and *Oedipus the King*.

PLAYS BASED ON MYTHS AND LEGENDS

To plan and write an exciting play based on a myth or legend, you need to spend time thinking about the story you'd like to tell, who's going to appear in it, and the shape of the story in your play. You also need to figure out what your characters will say to one another!

Ideas for your play

It's a great idea to write a play based on a myth or legend, as there are so many wonderful stories to bring to life. If you'd like to give it a try, don't limit yourself to myths and legends you already know.

There are amazing stories from a variety of cultures you could explore. You could start by reading a book of Greek or Roman myths and see if any of the stories appeal to you. There are also many American Indian myths and legends that you could act out. If you want to look for more unusual myths and legends, do some research into the ancient Egyptian, Aztec, or Indian civilizations.

This is the god of war, Huitzilopochtli, from an ancient Aztec myth.

Like many civilizations, the ancient Egyptians believed in a number of gods. They believed that the sun god Ra created the world. They had a goddess of the sky called Nut. The earth goddess was called Geb. Anubis was god of the dead, who had the head of a jackal.

The story of Theseus has been retold for centuries.

A story map for *Theseus and the Minotaur*

To create a play based on a myth or legend, you can start by making a story map for it. Here is an example for *Theseus and the Minotaur*:

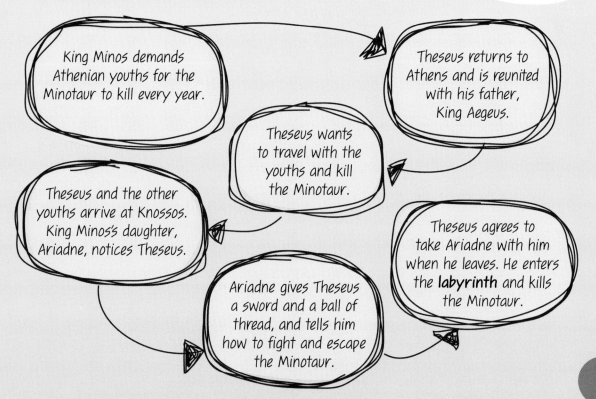

King Minos demands Athenian youths for the Minotaur to kill every year.

Theseus wants to travel with the youths and kill the Minotaur.

Theseus returns to Athens and is reunited with his father, King Aegeus.

Theseus and the other youths arrive at Knossos. King Minos's daughter, Ariadne, notices Theseus.

Ariadne gives Theseus a sword and a ball of thread, and tells him how to fight and escape the Minotaur.

Theseus agrees to take Ariadne with him when he leaves. He enters the **labyrinth** and kills the Minotaur.

Characters in a play based on a myth or legend

Myths and legends have particular types of characters. For example, the main character is usually a young, fearless hero. The story is about how he or she goes on a **quest** or completes a challenge. Often the hero has a fatal **flaw**, which can create problems or even lead to his or her downfall.

One example of a hero with a fatal flaw is Icarus. In Greek mythology, Icarus goes flying with his father, using wings they have made from seagull feathers that are attached to their arms with wax. Feeling invincible, Icarus ignores his father's warnings and flies too close to the Sun. The Sun's heat melts the wax holding his wings together, so Icarus falls into the sea.

Many myths and legends feature gods, goddesses, or other powerful figures who affect what happens to the hero. They can see what is happening in the world of humans and make decisions that can save or destroy them. Many such stories also feature terrible monsters, such as dragons and fearsome giants.

The trickster is a common character in myths and legends. For example, the coyote often appears as a trickster in many American Indian myths. It is the trickster's job to mislead the hero and cause trouble!

Characters in *Theseus and the Minotaur*

Once you've picked a myth or legend for your play, go through the story and make a list of the characters appearing in it. What **roles** do they play in the story? Are there any heroes, gods and goddesses, tricksters, or monsters in it? In *Theseus and the Minotaur*, you should have the following lead characters:

Theseus (the hero)
Brave but thoughtless; wants glory

King Minos (the villain)
The evil king who feeds young Athenians to the Minotaur

Ariadne (the helper)
Gives Theseus the tools and knowledge to defeat the Minotaur

Other characters:
King Aegeus, the prison guards, 6 Athenian boys, 7 Athenian girls, 1 (or more) **narrator**

The Minotaur (the monster)
Terrible beast that is feared by everyone; lives in a labyrinth

The plot of your play

When you base a play on an existing myth or legend, your job as playwright is easier because the **plot** has been written for you already! However, you may have to simplify the story. For example, a long myth with several strands might be too complicated for a play. You can simplify this by focusing on the main points of the story and leaving out any parts that aren't essential.

Another approach is to take a well-known myth or legend and adapt it in a new way. For example, the Norse god Thor and his enemy, Loki, have been characters in movies and TV shows such as *Thor* and *Avengers Assemble*.

The Norse god Loki changed shape and often caused mischief.

14

Setting the scene in *Theseus and the Minotaur*

You may want to include a narrator in your play. A narrator is useful—especially if your story is complicated—because he or she can give your audience the background to the story and help create the mythological setting of your play. A narrator can help to set the scene in *Theseus and the Minotaur* as follows:

NARRATOR: Welcome to the golden shores of the Aegean Sea! It is hard to imagine the horror that lies across the sea in Crete. Yet stories tell of a hideous monster, half-man, half-bull, lurking in a labyrinth. He is called the Minotaur! For two years, the king of Athens, Aegeus, has sent 14 young people to be eaten by this beast. If he refuses, King Minos will destroy his kingdom. It seems that all is lost.

A BEGINNING, MIDDLE, AND END

Just like all stories, the script for your play needs a shape. It needs a clear beginning, middle, and end.

Start by identifying the main scenes in the myth or legend you are using. Figure out what is most important in the story to help introduce the setting and characters. Is there any information you can leave out? What can you include at the beginning of your play so that the audience knows what the characters want?

It's now time to shape the story. Your play needs to move toward a point where the hero faces an obstacle or danger. You need to make sure there is plenty of **tension**!

Your myth or legend might include a fight scene.

As you move toward the end of the play, the hero will overcome the problem, and the story will be **resolved**. Remember, though, that there may not always be a happy ending in a myth or legend. Many plays based on myths or legends are tragedies, where the characters die or are left unhappy at the end.

The shape of *Theseus and the Minotaur*

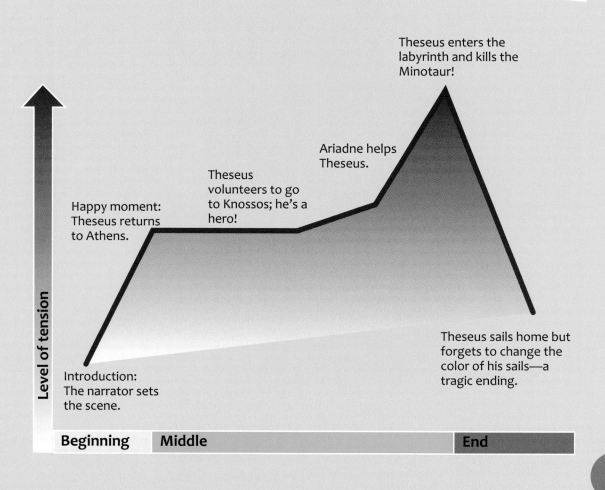

Theseus enters the labyrinth and kills the Minotaur!

Ariadne helps Theseus.

Theseus volunteers to go to Knossos; he's a hero!

Happy moment: Theseus returns to Athens.

Introduction: The narrator sets the scene.

Theseus sails home but forgets to change the color of his sails—a tragic ending.

Level of tension

Beginning **Middle** **End**

How your characters speak

When you write a play based on a myth or legend, you are retelling an ancient story that is hundreds or even thousands of years old. So you need to think carefully about the language you use. To give your play an authentic mythological feel, make sure your characters' dialogue doesn't sound too modern. How have writers of the other retellings made their characters speak? Research their methods and base your dialogue on what works for your play.

Try watching movies based on myths and legends and pay attention to how the dialogue has been written.

If there are gods and goddesses in your play, how could you make these characters speak so that they stand apart from the ordinary humans in your story? You could perhaps make the gods speak in a more **formal** language. Also, how would you make your hero stand out in the way he or she speaks? Since heroes can be adventurous and impatient, how likely are they to make long speeches or to speak in quick and short sentences, such as "Let's go!"? Snappy lines often add energy and a sense of excitement to a play.

A script for a play should give the actor instructions on how to act and speak.

Writing Tip

Remember, you can use stage directions to explain how your characters should act and speak. Use them for important moments in the play or when you want a character to do something specific. Don't include too many directions, though, as you also want your director and actors to feel confident to bring their own ideas to the play.

Dialogue in *Theseus and the Minotaur*
The dialogue below shows how you can **contrast** the language spoken by the hero and the villain:

KING MINOS: Young people of Athens, your feeble king, Aegeus, has sent you here because I demanded it. Your ruler and all Athenians must obey only me. I have brought you here to die at the hands of the Minotaur. Bow before me!

THESEUS: No more Athenians shall die!

KING MINOS: *(shouting)* Who is this rude person who refuses to bow before the most powerful king in all of Greece?

THESEUS: *(proudly)* I am Theseus, son of Aegeus. I am here to avenge the people of Athens!

WHO'S IN CHARGE?

Once you have written your script, you need to get a group of people together to bring the play to life!

A director's role

First, you need to choose someone to be the director. He or she will guide the process of turning a script into a performance. The director chooses which actors will play which **parts**. He or she will also lead **rehearsals** and guide the actors on how and when to speak and move. The director also works closely with the people behind the scenes, such as the **set** designer, the costume manager, the **props** manager, and the sound and lighting technicians.

A play based on a myth or legend might have some amazing costumes.

To be a director, you need to enjoy reading, especially scripts. You should have lots of experience working in a theater. You could start by assisting a director. A good director understands what everyone's job involves when a play is staged, so getting experience in acting and working backstage can be very helpful. You also need to be good at managing people and taking the lead in organizing all parts of staging a play.

Directing tips for *Theseus and the Minotaur*

If you are directing *Theseus and the Minotaur* yourself, below are some suggestions to help you do a great job:

1 Read the original myth and its related or backstories. For example, you could find out about Daedalus, who designed the labyrinth for the Minotaur, or read about where the Minotaur came from. The more you know about the world of your myth, the more you will understand what needs to be shown onstage.

2 Think about how you want the play to be performed. How will you bring the world of ancient Greece to life onstage? Think about the mood you want to create and how you could use color, scenery, costumes, lighting, and sound to do this. Talk to the backstage **crew** to see what ideas they have.

3 How will you show the Minotaur onstage? Will you use makeup or a mask? What about the sailing ships? Do some research to see how other people have staged similar myths.

4 Before you hold **auditions**, think about the main characters in the play. What type of actors would be best to play them?

Choosing roles for your actors

As the director, you should organize auditions to **cast** the play. People who want to act in the play are asked to read sections of the script and try out for different parts. You need to watch the actors' performances carefully and decide who would be best in which role.

Actors who are confident onstage and have strong, clear voices tend to make good heroes, gods, and goddesses. Actors playing the parts of monsters or mythical creatures need to be good at dance or gymnastics. They need to be comfortable moving around onstage.

This dramatic moment is from a play based on the book and movie of *How to Train Your Dragon*.

Think about the story of Theseus and the Minotaur. Whom do you know who would fit these parts?

Casting *Theseus and the Minotaur*

Below are some suggestions to help you choose the right actors for the roles:

The Minotaur
* No spoken lines onstage
* Choose an athletic actor who can learn how to fight onstage
* This is a good part for someone who likes the physical side of acting but doesn't want to learn any lines.

Theseus
* A brave leader and hero, but not without flaws
* The audience will support him when he enters the labyrinth to kill the Minotaur, but they may not like him so much when he abandons Ariadne
* Choose an actor who can easily show the positive and negative sides to this character.

King Minos
* A nasty, heartless character
* The actor who plays this part needs to be able to send chills down audiences' spines...

Ariadne
* Brave and determined, helpful to Theseus
* Is left devastated when Theseus abandons her at the end of the play
* Pick someone who can cover this whole range of emotions and feelings.

ACTING IN A PLAY BASED ON A MYTH OR LEGEND

When all of the actors have their parts, the team is ready to start rehearsing. As the director, you need to make sure the actors have all they need to do their job. For example, the director should help them to get to know their characters as well as the place where they will be performing.

Getting to know your character can be fun.

Getting to know the characters

Encourage your actors to read the original myth or legend so they are familiar with the story and the parts their characters play. If a movie of the story is available, you could watch it together. Afterward, talk about the characters and why they behave the way they do.

You could also try playing games to help your actors get into character. Try **improvising** the main scenes of the play. The actors could say words that come into their heads as they perform each stage of the story, without looking at the script. This will help them to understand what their characters want and how they are feeling.

Feel free to ask other actors tough questions about your characters.

"The Hot Seat"

Play this game to help the actors get to know all the characters in the play.

1. Get one of the characters—for example, Theseus—to sit on a chair, with the rest of the cast in a circle around this actor.

2. The cast members take turns to ask Theseus questions. Theseus should only answer by nodding or shaking his head. They should ask him lots of quick questions.

3. After a few minutes, the cast members could ask questions that Theseus has to answer in more detail.

4. When people start to run out of questions, put another character in the hot seat and start again.

5. After playing the game, share anything new you have learned about the characters with each other.

The ancient Greeks had to perform their plays by daylight, since they had no stage lighting.

Types of theater

Think about where you'd like to stage your play. The ancient Greeks usually performed in an amphitheater, where the audience would surround the stage on three or four sides. This makes the audience feel much closer to the action. If you pick a place like this, you must prepare your actors for it, as some people may find it scary to act so close to the audience. If you decide to perform your play outdoors, think about how you could use the space to help tell the story. For example, if you live near the ocean and your play is based on a myth about sea monsters, you could perform on the beach!

TRY IT

If your team gets tired with rehearsing, you could take a break from the script and go back to improvising the key scenes in the play. This will remind people what the other characters are thinking and feeling and freshen up the story again. You could even ask the actors to swap roles during improvisation, so they **empathize** more with each other.

Rehearsals can be fun.

Rehearsal time

Rehearsals begin with actors sitting together and reading the script. Then they move to the stage and start moving around, but they can still have the script with them. It is important that your actors continue learning and memorizing their lines outside of rehearsal time, so that they will eventually be able to perform without the script.

Make sure that any actors who are waiting offstage during rehearsals have something to do, so they don't get bored. Encourage them to quietly practice their lines with others. You could also leave copies of books on myths and legends backstage for people to read when they take a break. It's important to make sure the actors get used to being quiet backstage. They will need to do this during a performance!

BEHIND THE SCENES

Once you have decided where you'd like to perform your play, you need to think about how to set it up to create the right atmosphere. This means sorting out the set, costumes, props, lighting, and sound.

Designing and making a set

Your set is the **backdrop** to each scene and helps to show the audience where each part of the play is located. Professional theaters often use amazing sets with split-levels, moving parts, and other special mechanisms. However, it is possible to keep things simple and still end up with a nice-looking and effective set!

In ancient Greek theater, there was often a building or a tent called a *skene* behind the stage. This was painted to show the scene where the play was taking place, such as a temple. Actors playing gods and goddesses could go inside and then appear on the roof.

A few props can indicate time and place.

There are lots of ways to make a simple set. For example, you could paint scenery onto large boards, pieces of paper, or curtains that you can hang up at the back of the stage. If your myth or legend is set in a forest, then a green background with painted tree shapes will be effective. A play based on an ancient Egyptian myth could have pyramids and **hieroglyphics** painted onto the backdrop to set the scene.

There are lots of ways to create eye-catching sets.

Scenery in *Theseus and the Minotaur*

If you are staging a play based on the myth of Theseus and the Minotaur, you should probably include the following scenes:

Athens
* This appears at the start and the end of the play. You could show King Aegeus's palace, with pillars painted on stone-colored cloth.

Palace and dungeons of King Minos
* This scene needs to be darker and more sinister than those that take place in Athens. You could have a simple dark backdrop with a prison window.

The Labyrinth
You could show this by simply painting a maze onto the backdrop.

These actors are performing in a traditional Chinese opera.

Costumes

Someone on your team can be the costume manager. As the director, you can work with this person to make sure that your actors have the right clothes to wear when the play is performed.

Before making any decisions about costumes, think about the culture your story is based on. For example, if you're performing a Hindu myth, your characters should wear traditional Indian clothing. Look in reference books and on the Internet for ideas. It is handy to keep a scrapbook of pictures for reference. Alternatively, your actors could wear plain black clothing but wear simple masks, cloaks, or hats to make their characters stand apart.

Opera is a form of theater. Chinese opera involves singers in traditional costumes performing ancient Chinese myths and legends. The singers wear elaborate masks or makeup in colors that show the type of character they are playing. Gold and silver are used for a character who is a god or a demon. Green and yellow are negative colors that represent violence and cruelty. White represents evil, and purple is used for the heroes.

This actor is wearing a *chiton* and *peplos* (see below).

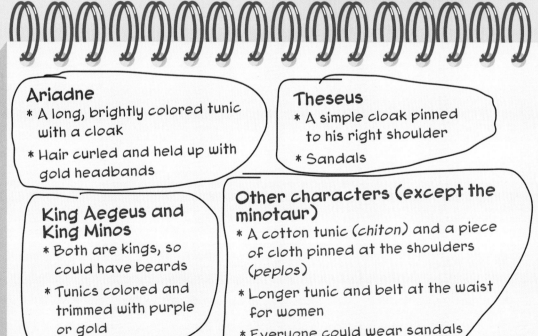

Ask your actors if they have any costumes at home. Maybe someone you know is good at making clothes and can help make costumes for you. You might be able to borrow something from other theaters or drama groups.

Costumes for *Theseus and the Minotaur*

Consider the following ideas for your actors:

Ariadne
* A long, brightly colored tunic with a cloak
* Hair curled and held up with gold headbands

King Aegeus and King Minos
* Both are kings, so could have beards
* Tunics colored and trimmed with purple or gold

Theseus
* A simple cloak pinned to his right shoulder
* Sandals

Other characters (except the minotaur)
* A cotton tunic (chiton) and a piece of cloth pinned at the shoulders (peplos)
* Longer tunic and belt at the waist for women
* Everyone could wear sandals

PORTRAYING THE MINOTAUR

You can portray a mythological monster like the Minotaur in your play using masks or shadow play.

Mask

This fits on the head of the actor playing the Minotaur.

1. Draw the shape of a bull's face on a piece of brown cardboard large enough to cover the actor's face. Cut this out.

2. Cut out eye holes so the actor can see.

3. You could cover the horns in a different type of cardboard or foil, to make them stand out.

4. Draw nostrils and eyebrows onto the bull's face.

5. Tie elastic onto the mask to fit on the actor's head.

You will need:
- brown sheet of cardboard
- silver or gold cardboard
- colored pens
- scissors
- a piece of elastic.

Shadow play

Alternatively, you could make a Minotaur shadow puppet.

You will need:
- black cardboard
- a light-colored pencil
- tape
- scissors
- a long stick
- a white sheet
- an overhead projector or a bright light.

1. Use the pencil to draw the outline of the Minotaur on a piece of black cardboard. The Minotaur should have a human body with the head of a bull. Make sure the horns are big enough to be seen clearly. You could cut out triangular-shaped holes for his eyes.

2. Cut out the Minotaur shape and tape it onto a stick.

3. When the Minotaur appears onstage, you will need to hang up a white sheet.

4. Behind the sheet (not in front of the audience!), shine an overhead projector or light onto the sheet. Place your Minotaur puppet in front of the light and move it around. Remember, the closer you place the puppet near the light source, the bigger its shadow on the sheet!

33

Props

Props are objects that the actors pick up and carry around onstage. There can be a lot of props in a play, so put a props manager in charge of organizing them and checking that nothing gets lost.

A play based on a myth or legend often involves interesting props, especially if the story you're telling is from another culture. Do some research beforehand so you know what your props should look like.

Many myths and legends involve fighting, so you might need weapons and armor. You can probably make these out of cardboard, but you could also buy plastic toy swords. It's important that nothing is too heavy or sharp—you don't want people getting hurt during a stage fight!

Alternatively, you could avoid using props altogether and get your actors to **mime** the actions instead. The actors can behave as if they are holding an object, and the audience simply imagines it is there.

These actors are using very simple, homemade props.

This ship was made for a production in a professional theater.

Props in *Theseus and the Minotaur*

Below are some ideas for the props you can include in your version of *Theseus and the Minotaur*:

- For the palace scenes, include props such as statues and vases to show the wealth of the kings.

- Have swords and spears for the guards who imprison Theseus and the other Athenian youths.

- Prepare a sword and a ball of string—these are what Ariadne gives to Theseus.

- Build a simple ship's mast with a black sail for the scenes when Theseus is traveling by sea.

THEATER JOB

Keep props organized so nothing is lost before an actor goes onstage. Usually a props manager has a props table backstage where every object is kept in the same place. The manager will check that everything is in place before a performance and after it ends, so people can find props easily the next time.

35

Lighting and sound

Using lighting and sound during a performance can add a lot to the atmosphere onstage. As the director, you need to find some technically minded people on your team to be in charge of these areas. They can work with you to decide what effects will be used.

The lighting engineer may use a complicated lighting system or just a few simple lights. This might depend on what is available in the theater and what his or her skills are. Make sure your lighting engineer explores the systems available. It would be useful for him or her to spend time finding out how everything works and what effects are possible. Make a note on the script of every lighting change, so you know what to expect.

When you shine a spotlight on a group of actors, you focus the audience's attention on them.

Playing drums is a simple way to create atmosphere.

The sound engineer also needs to follow the script closely to bring in different sounds and music at the right moments. In a play based on a myth or legend, it is very effective to use instruments or recorded music from the same culture as the story. For example, you could use a drum for an Indian myth.

Lighting in *Theseus and the Minotaur*
You will need bright lights for the sunlight in Athens. The stage could get gradually darker as Theseus arrives at Knossos and then is put in a cell. The dimmest lighting could be used for scenes inside the labyrinth—perhaps with a red color **filter** to make the stage more sinister. Use bright lights again for the end of the play. You could put a spotlight on Theseus when he realizes he has forgotten to change the sail and his father is dead.

The ancient Greeks used music during their theater performances. Many of their myths were originally sung to music. So, theaters continued this tradition, using **lyres**, pipes, and **percussion** instruments during plays.

THE FINAL STAGES

You are almost ready to perform your play! There are just a few final (but important) things to sort out. For example, you need to get people to come to watch your play. Also, you need to run final checks to make sure that everyone on the team knows what needs to be done.

Spreading the word

People need to know when and where your play is going to be staged. You need to **promote** your play. You can do this in a number of ways. Try contacting your local newspaper or radio station to see if they would be willing to mention your play. They will be interested to know if you have written and staged the play yourselves. You could ask for permission to hand out **fliers** about the play to students and parents at your school or around your local shopping center. You can also ask your family and friends to spread the word, too.

Take a photo of your Minotaur character to catch people's attention on fliers and posters.

title of play — **Theseus** and the **MINOTAUR**

Directed by Anthony Crawley — director

people playing the main characters

STARRING **BILL WHITE** as Theseus
RACHAEL SIM as Ariadne
BOB ROBERTS as The Minotaur

where and when the performance is

Wednesday, March 4—Saturday, March 7, at 8 p.m. at The Theater, Hill School

how you get tickets

E-mail main office for free tickets

Making a poster for your play

These are some important things to remember when making a poster:

- Do some research on the Internet or in the library and find a **font** that links to the myth or legend your play is based on—for example, USE A FONT LIKE THIS FOR A ROMAN MYTH!

- Use a large, dark font against a light background—this combination makes your text easier to read.

- Choose a striking image that shows a key moment from your play or one that sums up the message of the myth or legend. You could use a shadowy photo of the Minotaur's mask.

- Don't forget to include important information such as when and where the play will take place! Tell people if they need to buy or reserve tickets and how they do this.

- Finally, check your poster carefully to make sure that everything is correct before you print or photocopy it.

Final rehearsals

As you approach the date of your first performance, you should think about putting the finishing touches on your play. A director needs to arrange a **technical rehearsal** and a **dress rehearsal** for your team.

A technical rehearsal involves all the actors, but focuses on all the **cues** for the lights and sound effects in the play. At any point during the rehearsal, you can stop the action if you feel that certain parts need extra practice or if there are problems that still need to be solved.

It's important to rehearse in your costumes to get used to moving in unusual clothes.

A dress rehearsal is the final rehearsal before the first live performance. It involves running through the play as if it were an actual performance. All the costumes, props, lighting, sounds, and other special effects must be ready. If any mistakes are made, the cast must continue on as if in a real performance.

Some actors may get nervous toward the end of rehearsals and worry about forgetting their lines. It can be useful to pair actors up in the last couple of weeks and encourage them to help each other run through their lines. This extra practice can help them to relax a little.

Make sure you have allowed enough time to organize the printing of tickets and **programs**. You will also need people who are willing to work as your **front-of-house** helpers on the day of the performance, selling or giving tickets and programs to the audience.

TRY IT

There are certain things you should put in a program. For *Theseus and the Minotaur*, you could include:

- a short **synopsis** of the myth
- an explanation of why you chose to base your play on that myth
- some background about Greek theater
- a list of all the characters in the play, along with the names of the actors playing those parts
- the names and jobs of all the people working backstage
- photographs of the cast during rehearsals.

SHOWTIME!

The time has finally arrived to perform your play in front of an audience. It will have taken a lot of hard work by many people to reach this point, so make sure you enjoy yourselves!

Don't be scared of the audience! They are here to support you.

TRY IT

It's a good idea for actors to warm up before they go onstage. Try the following exercises. Get people to lie down, take deep breaths, and breathe out slowly. This will help make them feel calmer. Next, move on to a voice exercise. Get people to sit up straight, relax their jaws, and slowly say the sound "ah." Repeat this several times before moving on to other sounds, such as "ay" and "oh." Continue making these sounds as you stand up, then shake out your arms and legs.

Remember to bow when the audience claps at the end.

Your performance will go smoothly if everyone is organized and knows what is expected of him or her. As the director, it's a good idea for you to encourage your team to get a good night's sleep the night before the performance. It's important that everyone arrives on the day feeling fresh.

On the day, talk to everyone involved, from the lead actor to the person in charge of tickets, to check that everyone is clear on what needs to happen. While everyone is getting ready backstage, you could play a recording of some of the music from your play. This would help the cast get in the mood to perform.

If your actors are wearing stage makeup, it's a good idea to get some adults to help them put this on. Remember to put costumes on before the makeup, so that you don't smudge it!

When the curtain goes up, or the lights come on and the play begins, remember to have fun!

GLOSSARY

amateur not professional; done for fun

amphitheater semicircular open area with rows of seats

audition test for actors to try out for particular roles

backdrop background to a set

cast give actors roles in a play; the collective name for all the actors in a play

comedy type of entertainment that makes people laugh

contrast compare in order to show differences

crew people working backstage on a play

cue signal to an actor to move or speak

dialogue words actors speak

director person in charge of staging a play

dress rehearsal final rehearsal, run as if it is a performance

empathize understand the feelings of others

filter sheet that allows light to pass through it, but that may add color

flaw fault

flier small leaflet giving information

font set of letters and symbols in a particular design

formal following the expected rules

front-of-house area of the theater business concerning the audience, such as ticket sales

hieroglyphics symbols used in ancient Egyptian writing

improvising making up a sketch as you go along

labyrinth another word for a maze

legend traditional story that may be based on real events

line sentence of dialogue in the script

lyre stringed instrument like a harp

mime act without using words

minotaur monster from Greek myths that is shaped half like a man and half like a bull

myth very old, traditional story that is often about gods and the creation of the world

narrator person who describes and explains what is happening

oral spoken

part role in a play

percussion instrument that is played by the musician hitting it

playwright person who writes the text of the play

plot story of a book, movie, or play

program booklet for audience members giving information about the play, cast, and crew

promote encourage people to like or do something

prop object that actors can move around onstage

quest mission or task

rehearsal session held to practice a play

resolve reach the point where all the obstacles in the play are overcome

role character or part in a play

script text of the play

set scenery and furniture on the stage

stage direction instruction for an actor in the script of a play

synopsis summary of a story

technical rehearsal practice that focuses on sound, lighting, and use of props

tension emotional strain and stress

tragedy serious play with a sad ending

FIND OUT MORE

Web sites

FactHound offers a safe, fun way to find Internet sites related to this book. All of the sites on FactHound have been researched by our staff.

Here's all you do:

Visit www.facthound.com
Type in this code: 9781484627723

Most cities and many towns have theater companies that put on plays for kids. Do research to find the theaters near you that offer plays for kids or theater training for young people. Perhaps you could ask if you could visit and look around, or ask about plays that are coming up. Check to see if there are any workshops with the actors or the writers.

Plays to read

Think about some interesting myths and legends or stories inspired by them, such as *How to Train Your Dragon* or American Indian legends. With an adult's help, you can find different stage adaptations of these stories. If you visit your local library, you can also find new plays you haven't heard of that feature myths and legends.

Drama game

If you enjoyed the "Hot Seat" improvisation game earlier in the book, perhaps try the following improvisation game, too.

"I Am a Caterpillar"

First, set a stopwatch for the game to last ten minutes. Then, try moving around as a caterpillar. To help you keep in the mood, you could be repeating "I am a caterpillar." Meet another "caterpillar" and ask if it would like to play a game, as follows:

1. Both people in the pair should put their hands behind their back.

2. They should count to five and then hold up a number of their fingers on both hands.

3. The first person to tell the other one how many fingers the other is holding up moves up to the "next level." They can become a chrysalis.

4. The other, losing, caterpillar remains a caterpillar.

5. This is repeated with another person.

6. Here, the winner becomes a butterfly, and the loser becomes a caterpillar again.

7. When two butterflies meet, one of them will win and will remain as this character. The losing butterfly goes back to being a chrysalis. At the end of the ten minutes, talk about what you think of the game.

INDEX

actors 6, 8, 19, 20, 22–27, 41, 42
acts 17
American Indian myths and legends 7, 10, 12
amphitheaters 6, 26
ancient Egyptians 11, 28
ancient Greeks 4, 6, 8, 26, 28, 37
Arthur, King 4, 5
auditions 21, 22
Aztec myths 10

backstories 21
backstage crew 20, 21

casting 23
characters 8, 12–13, 18, 21
Chinese myths and legends 7, 30
Chinese opera 30
comedies 8
costume managers 20, 30
costumes 30–31, 40, 41, 43
cues 40

dance 22
dialogue 8, 18–19
directors 6, 19, 20–23, 24, 36, 43
dress rehearsals 40, 41
drums 37

empathizing 26
endings 16

fatal flaws 12, 23
fight scenes 16, 23, 34
fliers 38
fonts 39
formal language 18

front-of-house people 41

gods and goddesses 4, 5, 8, 10, 11, 12, 18, 22, 28
Greek mythology 4, 7, 12, 14
gymnastics 22

heroes 4, 8, 12, 13, 16, 18, 19, 22, 23
"Hot Seat" game 25
How to Train Your Dragon 7, 22, 47

ideas for a play 10–11
improvisation 24, 26

legends: what they are 4
lighting 20, 36, 37, 40
lines, learning 27

makeup 21, 30, 43
masks 21, 30, 32
Midas, King 4
mime 34
monsters 12, 13, 22, 32–33
movies 7, 14, 18, 24
Mulan 7
music 37
myths: what they are 4

narrators 14, 15
nervousness 41
Norse mythology 5, 7, 14

open-air theaters 6, 26
opening night 42–43
oral storytellers 4

Percy Jackson 7, 14
photos 38, 41

playwrights 6, 8
plots 14
posters 39
programs 41
promoting your play 38–39
props 34–35
props managers 20, 34, 35
props tables 35

rehearsals 20, 27, 40–41

scenes 16, 17
scripts 6, 8–9, 16–17, 21, 27
set design 28–29
set designers 20
shadow puppets 33
Sophocles 8, 9
sound 20, 37, 40
spotlights 36, 37
stage directions 9, 19
story maps 11
structuring the script 16–17
synopsis 41

technical crew 20, 36–37
technical rehearsals 40
tension 16
Theseus and the Minotaur 11, 13, 15, 17, 19, 21, 23, 29, 31, 35, 37, 41
ticket sales 39
tragedies 8, 9, 16
tricksters 12

Vikings 5
villains 13, 19, 23

warm-up exercises 42